Click, Click

Click, Click
© 1999 Creative Teaching Press, Inc.
Written by Margaret Allen, Ph.D.
Illustrated by Dave Clegg
Project Director: Luella Connelly
Editor: Joel Kupperstein
Art Director: Tom Cochrane

Published in the United States of America by:
Creative Teaching Press, Inc.
P.O. Box 6017
Cypress, CA 90630-0017

CTP 2907

Rick and Mack packed for a trip.

"Tuck it in the backpack," said Gram.

3

Rick and Mack ran to the rocks.
"Kick the rocks, Rick," said Mack.

Quick, Gram.
Get the bug on the stick!

Click, click went Gram. "I got it!"

Rick and Mack ran to the pond.
"Quack, quack," said the ducks.

7

Quick, Gram.
Get the ducks on the deck!

Click, click went Gram. "I got it!"

Rick and Mack ran to the sand.

Quick, Gram.
Get the buck at the pan!

Click, click went Gram. "I got it!"

Rick and Mack ran to the mat.
Rick and Mack sat.

Quick, quick, Rick and Mack.
Get Gram on the mat!

Click, click went Rick and Mack.
"We got it!"

BOOK 7: Click, Click

Focus Skills: qu, ck

Focus-Skill Words		Sight Word	Story Words
quack	ki**ck**	we	Gram
quick	Ma**ck**		trip
ba**ck**pa**ck**	pa**ck**ed		
bu**ck**	Ri**ck**		
cli**ck**	ro**ck**s		
de**ck**	sti**ck**		
du**ck**s	tu**ck**		

Focus-Skill Words contain a new skill or sound introduced in this book.

Sight Words are among the most common words encountered in the English language (appearing in this book for the first time in the series).

Story Words appear for the first time in this book and are included to add flavor and interest to the story. They may or may not be decodable.

Interactive Reading Idea

Reread the story and have your young reader find these words: *buck, duck, rock,* and *stick*. Next, have your reader draw and label a *buck, a duck, a rock,* and a *stick*.